PowerKids Readers:
Nature Books™

Snow

Kristin Ward

The Rosen Publishing Group's
PowerKids Press™
New York

For Thomas and Mak, with love

Published in 2000 by The Rosen Publishing Group, Inc.
29 East 21st Street, New York, NY 10010

First Edition
Book design: Michael de Guzman
Photo Credits: p. 1 © Andre Jenny/International Stock; p. 5 CORBIS/Ric Ergenbright; p. 7 © John Terence Turner/FPG International; p. 9 © Alan Kearney/FPG International; p. 11 © Scott Barrow/International Stock; p. 13 © Caroline Wood/International Stock; p. 15 © Stockman/International Stock; p. 17 © Michael Philip Manheim/International Stock; p. 19 CORBIS/Stuart Westmorland; p. 21 © Norris Clark/International Stock.

Ward, Kristin.
    Snow / by Kristin Ward.
    p. cm. — (Nature books)
Includes index.
Summary: Describes snow's appearance and composition, and what kids can do in the snow.
ISBN 0-8239-5529-X (lib. bdg.)
1. Snowflakes—Juvenile literature. [1. Snowflakes.] I. Title. II. Series: Nature books (New York, N.Y.)
QC926.37.W37 1999
551.57'84—dc21

                                        98-49734
                                           CIP
                                           AC

Manufactured in the United States of America

Contents

Snow falls from clouds in
the sky.
Snow falls when it is cold
outside.
Snow is frozen water.

5

Snowflakes are white.
Snowflakes are cold and
wet.

Snowflakes are different shapes.
They are different sizes, too.

Sometimes it snows a little.

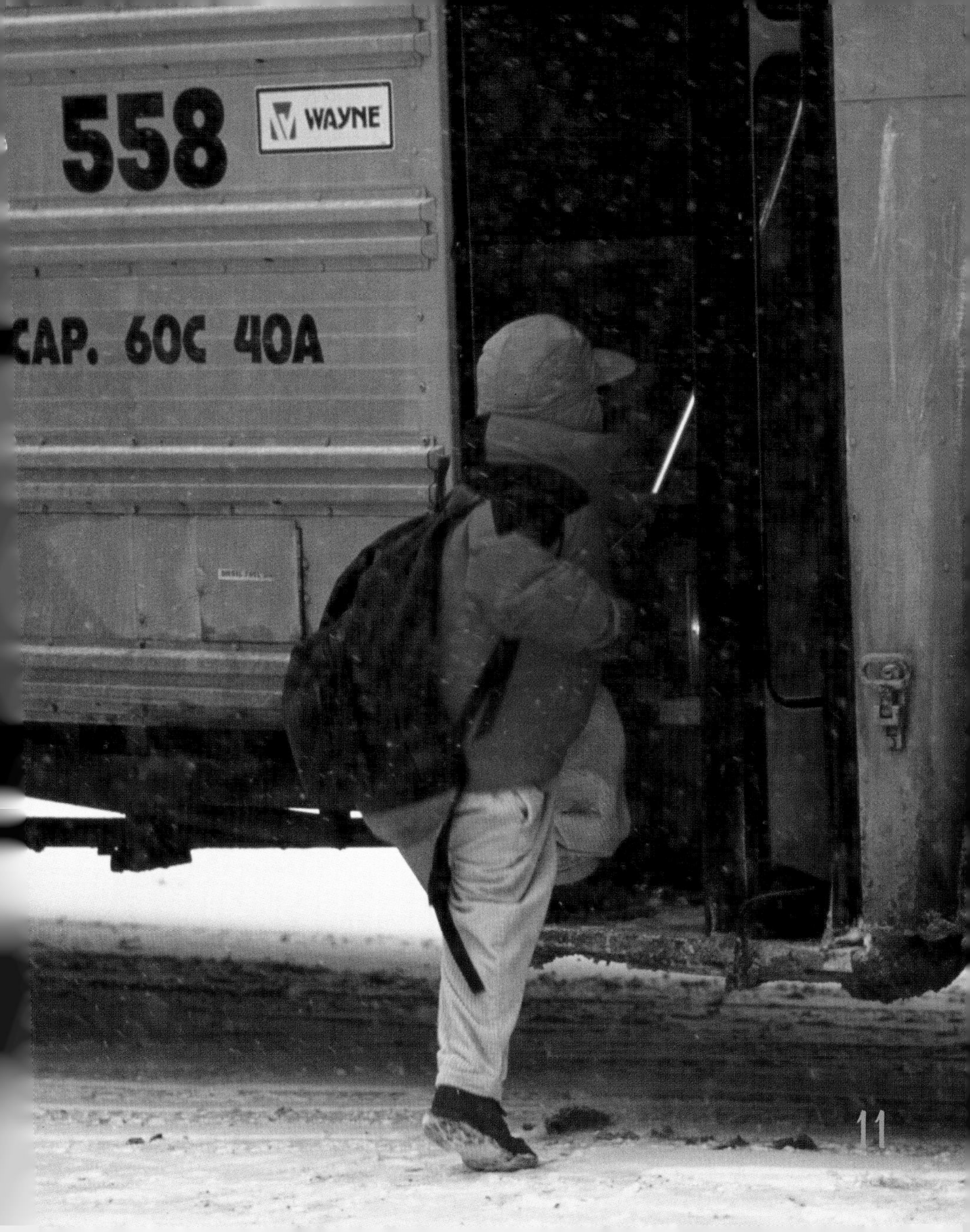
558
WAYNE
CAP. 60C 40A

Sometimes it snows a lot.

Special trucks are used to move snow.
They are called snowplows.

You can build things with snow.

You can build a snowman.

You can build a snow
house.

You can even go for a ride on the snow.

Words to Know

CLOUDS   SNOW

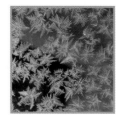 

SNOWFLAKE   SNOWPLOW

SNOWMAN

Here are more books to read about snow:
Snowflakes, Sugar, and Salt: Crystals Up Close (Science All Around You)
by Chu Maki, photographs by Isamu Sekido
Lerner Publications

Web Sites:

Due to the changing nature of Internet links, PowerKids Press has developed an online list of Web sites related to the subject of this book. This site is updated regularly. Please use this link to access the list:
www.powerkidslinks.com/nature/snow/

Index

Word Count: 83

Note to Librarians, Teachers, and Parents

PowerKids Readers (Nature Books) are specially designed to help emergent and beginning readers build their skills in reading for information. Simple vocabulary and concepts are paired with photographs of real kids in real-life situations or stunning, detailed images from the natural world around them. Readers will respond to written language by linking meaning with their own everyday experiences and observations. Sentences are short and simple, employing a basic vocabulary of sight words, as well as new words that describe objects or processes that take place in the natural world. Large type, clean design, and photographs corresponding directly to the text all help children to decipher meaning. Features such as a contents page, picture glossary, and index help children get the most out of PowerKids Readers. They also introduce children to the basic elements of a book, which they will encounter in their future reading experiences. Lists of related books and Web sites encourage kids to explore other sources and to continue the process of learning.